T009797C

Soul of Kyoto

A GUIDE TO 30 EXCEPTIONAL EXPERIENCES

WRITTEN BY THIERRY TEYSSIER
PHOTOS BY ITO MAKOTO AND EBISU SHIN
ILLUSTRATED BY FAUSTINE FERRARA

JONGLEZ PUBLISHING

Travel guides

*'ONE AFTERNOON UNDER
A CHERRY TREE IN KYOTO AND
I'M LIFTED TO THE HEIGHTS OF
THE INTOXICATION OF EXISTENCE.'*

RENÉ DEPESTRE

Kyoto is a special city, which, like Japan as a whole, will never leave you cold. You'll either love it or hate it – never anything in between!

It's also a city that holds many secrets and isn't as easy to discover as you might think.

And that's precisely what makes it so appealing: every day spent in Kyoto promises to deliver a wealth of surprises and encounters. You could spend ten years here and still discover hidden places while taking a walk, during a conversation, or on an outing with friends.

In order to respect and understand this unique city, you have to accept that you'll need to slow down your frantic pace and give in to the unhurried tempo of the locals.

Visiting Kyoto is all about breathing first, then observing, and finally feeling. Only then will Kyoto open up to you, filling you with a sense of wonder.

WHAT YOU WON'T FIND
IN THIS GUIDE

- a list of the city's museums
- where to see a geisha show
- how to get to the top of Kyoto Tower

WHAT YOU WILL FIND
IN THIS GUIDE

- the best place to picnic along the river without being attacked by eagles
- where to get your own barbecue grilled behind the fish market
- a private home where you can experience the tea ceremony
- the artisan who is reviving traditional Kyoto fans
- a restaurant hidden in a temple
- the city's best egg sandwich
- public baths transformed into a café
- the aburi mochi at the root of a thousand-year-old rivalry

SYMBOLES USED IN
'SOUL OF KYOTO'

< 40 euros

40 to 80 euros

> 80 euros

They don't speak English here,
so if a reservation is required,
ask your hotel (or a Japanese
friend) to help you.

100% traditional
Japan

You'll often need to show your taxi driver
the addresses in this guide, so we've included
them in Japanese on each page.

30 EXPERIENCES

GOLDEN PAVILLON KINKAKUJI

NIJO-JC CASTLE

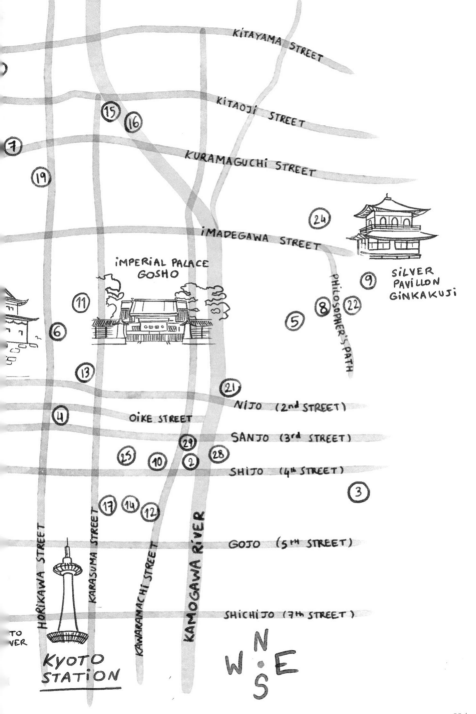

受付

HAVE YOUR FISH GRILLED
AT THE MARKET

In Japan, barbecuing is an institution. Whether at home or in the biggest restaurants, it remains one of the pillars of Japanese gastronomy.

For a proper reunion with friends, there are places like this where you can bring whatever you feel like grilling.

Treat yourself: take advantage of the market alleys out back to pick up whatever strikes your fancy, or let the host create dishes for you to grill.

Good to know: though relatively quiet during the week, this place gets very lively on weekends.

 BBQ COURT 339
(KABUSHIKIGAISHA SANSAKU)
74 SUJAKUHOZOCHO, SHIMOGYO-KU

京都市下京区 朱雀宝蔵町 74

| DAILY: 11am / 10pm | +81 12-047-8339 | bbq.339.co.jp |

KYOTO'S
SPEAKEASY

It may be located in the heart of the Pontocho district, but you probably won't find it if you're searching for a bar. So try a bookstore instead – you'll have better luck.

Need another clue? Look for a yellow door. Behind it, you'll find the best cocktails in town, hands down.

 BEE'S KNEES
364 KAMIYACHO, NAKAGYO-KU

京都市中京区 紙屋町 364
マツヤビル 1F

MON–THU: 6pm / 1am
FRI & SAT: 6pm / 2am   +81 75-585-5595   bees-knees-kyoto.jp
SUN: Closed

SPEND A NIGHT
IN A JAPANESE GARDEN

Between the extremely strict ryokans, which we don't recommend for more than a night, and the big international hotels, it isn't easy to find the hotel of your dreams in Kyoto.

And then, one day, you hear about Sowaka: finally, a nice place in the city's historic center for a rest between seeing the sights … with the added bonus that the welcome and service they offer will transport you straight to the heart of Japanese hospitality.

 SOWAKA HOTEL
480 KIYOICHO, YASAKA TORIIMAE-SAGARU,
SHIMOGAWARA-DORI, HIGASHIYAMA-KU

京都市東山区下河原通八坂鳥居前下
ル清井町480

+81 75-541-5323　　　　sowaka.com

A GLASS OF WINE
FROM THE MORNING

Here's a place that has spared a thought for those unfortunate jetlagged foreigners who find themselves wandering around in a daze, not knowing whether it's morning, afternoon, or the middle of the night.

Tarel is the first wine bar that's already open in the morning and also serves coffee. And the owner bakes his own bread. Stopping by for lunch on the go is also a good idea.

📍 **TAREL**
130 SHIKIAMICHO, SHIKIAMI CONCON 01,
NAKAGYO-KU

京都市中京区 式阿弥町 130

DAILY: 11am / 7pm

Check Instagram for closures, which change regularly:
@tarel_kyoto

TREAT YOURSELF
TO A KYOTO FAN

At the end of a little alley where you'd least expect it, there's a very special fan workshop: Hachiya Uchiwa, which has chosen to specialize in the instantly recognizable shape of Kyoto's traditional fans.

This workshop represents a true rebirth of the craft, since the last one like it disappeared almost 50 years ago.

Just choose the papers you want and watch your fan take shape before your astonished eyes.

HACHIYA UCHIWA
40 SHISHIGATANI
HONENIN NISHIMACHI,SAKYO-KU

京都市左京区鹿ヶ谷法然院西町40

SAT & SUN: 10am / 5pm

info@hachiya-uchiwa.jp
instagram: @hachiya_uchiwa

SONGBIRD FUCKIN COFFEE

**SONGBIRD COFFEE
NAKAGYOKU TAKEYACHODOORI
HORIKAWA HIGASHIIRI
NISHITAKEYACHO 529, 2nd floor**

中京区竹屋町通堀川東入ル
西竹屋町529

FRI–WED: 11am / 8pm
THU, 1st & 3rd WED of the month:
Closed

+81 75-252-2781

songbird-design.jp/webstore

AN UNFORGETTABLE
EGG SANDWICH

Japanese students know where it's at: when they want an egg sandwich, they head over to Songbird. Don't hesitate to follow their lead for a good quick meal.

This is the three-star version of the top-selling item in Kyoto's convenience stores.

FOR STATIONERY
LOVERS

Needless to say, with a culture that values writing and drawing, Kyoto has no shortage of stationery studios. But if you're looking for the rarest of papers, be sure not to miss this one.

A studio that feels timeless, Kamisoe creates papers each of which is more beautiful than the next. They'll make you want to grab a pen and start writing, pronto.

 KAMISOE
11-1 MURASAKINO HIGASHIFUJINOMORICHO,
KITA-KU

京都市北区紫野東藤ノ森町
11-1

| TUE-SUN: noon / 6pm | +81 75-432-8555 | kamisoe.com |
| MON: Closed | | |

THE BEST PIZZA
IN TOWN

Japanese pizza? Yes, it exists, and it's worth a trip to Monk, the restaurant of your dreams, a subtle mix of Japanese gastronomy and international culinary technicality – or maybe it's the other way around?

The menu at Monk is incredible and will never cease to amaze you. It's the best pizza in town, revamped with Japanese ingredients that will sweep you away with their surprising and subtle flavors: venison, mackerel, shirasu, and even glazed eggplant ...

Ask the chef to do you the favor of cutting each pizza into slices so you can enjoy the privilege of tasting them all.

MONK
147 JODOJI SHIMOMINAMIDACHO,
SAKYO-KU

京都市左京区浄土寺下南田町147

TUE–SAT: 5pm / 11pm (last service 8:30pm)
SUN & MON: Closed

+81 75-748-1154

restaurant-monk.com

MEDITATE IN
A SECRET TEMPLE

With 1,600 Buddhist temples and nearly 400 Shinto shrines, Kyoto leaves the choice of which ones to visit up to you. But let your steps guide you beyond the most famous places, like the Golden or Silver Pavilion, to some that are less conspicuous but no less interesting.

Honen-in is one of them. The peace and quiet of this little-known temple give visitors a chance to rest, breathe, and meditate. Gratitude awaits at the end of the road – or rather, at the bend in its wonderful gardens.

 HONEN-IN
30 SHISHIGATANI GOSHONODANCHO, SAKYO-KU　　京都市左京区鹿ヶ谷御所ノ段町 30

| DAILY: 6am / 4pm | +81 75-771-2420 | honen-in.jp |

IT'S
DOUGHNUT TIME

When architects and designers oversee the creation of an ethical and responsibly sourced doughnut, the result is explosive: your taste buds will remember it for a long time to come.

Even the flour is produced in the laboratory right in front of you. And if you don't see anything in the wide selection of doughnuts-to-go that hits the spot, take a seat and order one made-to-order and plated. Deee-licious.

 KOÉ DONUTS
557 NAKANOCHO, SHINKYOGOKU-DORI
SHIJO-AGARU, NAKAGYO-KU

京都府京都市中京区新京極通四
条上ル中之町五五七番地

| DAILY: 8am / 8pm | +81 75-748-1162 | koe.com/koedonuts |

A SAKE BAR
IN A LUMBER YARD

An *izakaya* that pops up in a lumber yard after office hours?

In Kyoto, no big deal.

Ikura Mokuzai will treat you to his barbecued tuna belly amidst a jumble of wood planks that never could have imagined they were destined for such a good time.

SAKABA IKURA MOKUZAI
77-1 YABUNOUCHICHŌ,
SHIMOCHOJAMACHI-DORI
NISHINOTŌIN-HIGASHIIRU, KAMIGYŌ-KU

京都市上京区下長者町通西洞院
東入 藪之内町77-1

MON–SAT: 5pm / 10pm
SUN AND PUBLIC HOLIDAYS: Closed

+81 90-9848-0995

Instagram @sakaba_ikuramokuzai

MATCHA TEA
DONE DIFFERENT

Coffee shops are trendy all around the world ... and then there's Yugen in Kyoto.

Imagine a coffee shop, replace the coffee with tea, and hey presto! Welcome to an establishment that manages to combine the best ancient traditions with the zeitgeist of today. Gorgeous products offered in a breathtakingly modern ambience.

A bit of advice: order two of whatever you're having right off the bat because you're sure to want seconds anyway.

YUGEN
266-2 DAIKOKU-CHO,
SHIMOGYO-KU

京都府 京都市下京区 大黒町 266-2

DAILY: 11am / 7pm   +81 75-606-5062   yugen.liv-japan.com

1

2

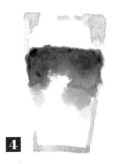

3

THE EPITOME OF
JAPANESE
CRAFTMANSHIP

YDS is an art gallery that combines exhibition spaces with a selection of items for sale.

The owners spend part of each year crisscrossing Japan in search of the most out-of-the-way artisans and the rest of it sharing its treasures with you.

This traditional family-run place is magnificent, the selection meticulous, and every moment here unique. Make sure to take the time to visit every floor.

YDS SHOP & GALLERY
717 NIJOSHINCHO, SHINMACHI-DORI
NIJO-AGARU, NAKAGYO-KU

中京区新町通二条上ル二条新町717

| TUE–SAT: 11am / 6pm SUN, MON, 2nd SAT of each month, and Public Holidays: Closed | +81 75-211-1664 | takahashitoku.com/yds |

FILL YOUR SUITCASE
WITH SWEETS

A treat for the eyes as much as for the taste buds, Crochet's multicolored candy is the ideal gift to bring back from Kyoto.

Everything is perfect in this tiny store, all the way down to the packaging, which is sure to surprise more than a few people. A true concentrated dose of Japan.

CROCHET
69 SHIOYACHO, AYANOKOJI-DORI
TOMINOKOJI-HIGASHIIRU,
SHIMOGYO-KU

京都市下京区綾小路富小路東入塩屋町69

WED–SUN: 10am / 7pm
MON & TUE: closed

+81 75-744-0840

crcht.com

クロッシェ

kyoto

京あめ

A COFFEE SHOP
IN THE LAND OF TEA

Wife & Husband has a three-word philosophy: coffee, antiques, and picnics. This one-of-a-kind place allows you to enjoy the first while browsing the second, before renting everything you need to enjoy an outdoor lunch in spring.

When asked 'So, what's next?', the owners shrug. Indeed, they have discovered a recipe for happiness in this tiny, cozy space on the ground floor of their home, with its meticulously roasted coffee and to-die-for cheese-and-honey toast that requires no further tweaking.

N.B: seating capacity is limited, so there may be a bit of a wait outside. An opportunity to learn to appreciate, like a true Japanese, that waiting only enhances your pleasure.

 WIFE & HUSBAND
106-6 KOYAMA SHIMOUCHIKAWARACHO,
KITA-KU

京都市北区小山下内河原町106-6

DAILY: 10am / 5pm
(check website for closing days)
Picnic service ends at 3pm

+81 75-201-7324

wifeandhusband.jp

67

- WIFE & HUSBAND -

THE EMBLEMATIC KYOTO COUPLE WIFE & HUSBAND RUN A COFFEE SHOP
UNLIKE ANY OTHER, WHOSE CALM AND SERENE ATMOSPHERE
BLENDS ALL THE FLAVORS OF JAPANESE PHILOSOPHY.

INTERVIEW

How did you get the idea for Wife & Husband?

Ikumi: Ever since I was a little girl, I've always wanted to have a store of my own, even though my parents would have preferred for me to think about other things!

Kyoichi: The idea for the coffee shop came to us very naturally. We knew what we wanted to share: coffee, the antiques we love, and the art of picnicking! In fact, it isn't a concept, it's our life philosophy. We love coffee, antiques, and enjoying time by the river. Why not devote our lives to that? We weren't looking to open our coffee shop on a street with a lot of traffic to ensure we'd be successful; in fact, that wasn't our goal at all ... We simply opened it in our own house.

You told me that you yourselves designed the coffee shop ...

K: Yes, the whole thing. We love antiques, so it seemed natural to design the store ourselves.

I: We like to care for antique objects. And we don't like today's society: buy, consume, throw away. We don't agree with it.

K: All our customers want to buy our objects! That's why we decided to open a gallery.

Picnicking is the third part of your philosophy. Why is that?
I: It stems from the same feeling: we weren't comfortable with take-away and the waste it creates.

K: Since we love spending time by the river more than anything else, we decided to take advantage of the fact that it's nearby to rent out returnable picnicking items to our customers. We're not in Paris, where we'd be able to have outdoor seating. Offering picnics by the river was our way of expanding our tiny café while sharing a place we love.

Do you still manage to enjoy Kyoto?
I: Yes, though less often now that we have children. I think it's important to teach them to share moments like these.

How would you describe your city?
K: I grew up in Kobe but came to Kyoto to study. I fell in love with the city and decided to stay! Kyoto is compact. Even so, the city offers many spaces for living, and nature is present everywhere. Living here allows you to appreciate and enjoy the balance between all the elements.
I: The urban planning regulations are very strict in Kyoto. There are no enormous buildings, and you can see the mountains from everywhere. When you're down by the river, the sky is vast.

What experiences would you like to share with the readers of *Soul of Kyoto*?
I: Picnicking by the river! (laughs) I really like going for walks by the Shimogamo shrine as well.
K: The botanical garden is wonderful.

After your coffee shop, antiques store, and coffee roastery, what's next for you?
Nothing! We only opened the roastery because our needs were growing, and we had to be respectful of our neighborhood and not become a nuisance by causing smoke and odors. But we've accomplished everything we wanted to. We don't need anything else.

A PICNIC
BY THE RIVER

A trip to Kyoto isn't complete without a picnic by the Kamo River, with your feet in the grass.

But take care when choosing your spot: the eagles that keep boaters company are as greedy as they are majestic, and it's never fun to have your sandwich snatched out of your hand by a hooked beak you didn't hear coming.

How to avoid them? Head over to Wife & Husband (see page 64) to rent all the necessary equipment and then settle down nearby – the eagles don't congregate along this stretch of the river.

WIFE & HUSBAND
106-6 KOYAMASHIMOUCHIKAWARACHO,
KITA-KU

京都市北区小山下内河原町106-6

| DAILY: 10am / 5pm (check website for closing days) Picnic service ends at 3pm | +81 75-201-7324 | wifeandhusband.jp |

D&DEPARTMENT
397 SHINKAICHO, TAKAKURA-DORI
BUKKOJI-SAGARU,
SHIMOGYO-KU

京都市下京区高倉通仏光寺下ル新開町397
本山佛光寺内

THU–MON: 11am / 6pm		
TUE & WED: Closed	+81 75-343-3217	d-department.com
Last orders at 5pm		

A CONCEPT STORE
IN THE HEART OF A TEMPLE

When you ask, 'Where can I find a really good concept store in Kyoto?', you probably don't expect to be directed to … a temple.

And yet, D&Department is the best answer: in the heart of a temple, a boutique, tea room/restaurant, and exhibition space welcome you solicitously.

The icing on the cake? They also have a publishing house, whose poetic offerings are well worth lingering over.

PICK ONE SIDE
OF THE STREET
TO ENJOY SOME *MOCHI*

Imagine a family that, over a thousand years ago, decides to create a unique spot for eating *aburi mochi*, those delicious rice cakes glazed with miso.

An instant success, the business thrives. So much so that, a few centuries later, a cousin chooses to open a competing business with the same unique recipe ... directly across the street.

Ever since, each generation of Kyotoites has had to choose between these two establishments – and stick with it – to enjoy the city's best aburi mochi.

 **ICHIWA ABURI MOCHI
69 MURASAKINO IMAMIYACHO,
KITA-KU**

京都府京都市北区紫野今宮町 69

| THU–TUE: 10am / 5pm WED: Closed | +81 75-492-6852 | Facebook あぶり餅　一和（一文字屋和輔） |

77

19

GET A KIMONO
CUSTOM MADE

Kimonos and *yukatas*, here we come!

Hinodeya is one of Kyoto's most reputable clothing boutiques.

Come in and treat yourself: they'll make whatever traditional Japanese clothing you want with the fabrics of your choice.

They'll even be so kind as to send them to you anywhere in the world. Can't decide on a season? We suggest having outfits made for all four ...

HINODEYA
106 KEIKAINCHO, OMIYA-DORI
TERANOUCHI-SAGARU, KAMIGYO-KU

京都市上京区大宮通り寺ノ内下がる
花開院町106

MON–FRI: 10am / 6pm
SAT: 10am / 6pm
SUN: Closed

+81 75-441-1437

hinodeya.co.jp
Instagram @hinodeya1868

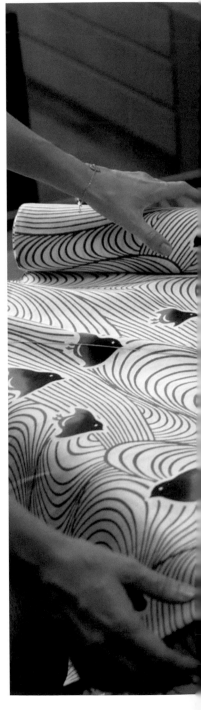

20

A CREATIVE WORKSHOP
BEHIND THE FISH
MARKET

Is it really true that the world's greatest inventions are born in garages? Here's one that will prove it to you.

Hidden away in the alleys behind the fish market, Kyoto Makers Garage invites you on a creative escape for a few hours. There's a 3D printer, a laser cutting machine ...

Just add the spark of your imagination.

 KYOTO MAKERS GARAGE
73-1 SUJAKUHOZOCHO, SHIMOGYO-KU

京都市下京区朱雀宝蔵町73-1
ライトワンビル1F

| SAT–WED: 10am / 7pm THU & FRI: Closed | +81 75-205-5319 | kyotomakersgarage.com |

THE BEST DESSERTS
IN KYOTO

A very discreet tea room and a display case of pastries-to-go –
there's nothing about this place that seems particularly special.
But the secret lies in the plated desserts, which Satomi Fujita
will prepare to order and which are as delicate as their creator.

Delightful tidbits of texture and flavor for guilt-free indulgence.

 KASHIYA
270-3 YOSHINAGACHO, SAKYO-KU   京都府京都市左京区吉永町270-3

| WED–MON: 11:30am / 7pm
TUE: Closed | +81 75-708-5244 | Instagram @kashiya_kyoto |

A STOP ALONG
THE PHILOSOPHER'S WALK

A stroll along the Philosopher's Walk is a must before or after visiting the Silver Pavilion, especially if you're lucky enough to be here in spring when the cherry trees are in bloom.

But there's another treasure along this path that's open all year round: Artech.

Ceramics, wood, lacquer, metal ... The selection of Japanese handicrafts on offer here is so exceptional you'll want to splurge at every stall.

KISO ARTECH
43 SHISHIGATANI HONENINCHO, SAKYO-KU

京都市左京区鹿ケ谷法然院町43

| DAILY: 9:30am / 5:30pm (Check website for closing days) | +81 75-751-7175 | kiso-artech.co.jp |

- GO ON PROJECT -

THE JOINT EFFORT OF SIX CREATIVES, THE GO ON PROJECT IS ROOTED IN TRADITIONAL CRAFTS AND BRANCHES OUT INTO MULTIPLE FIELDS, INCLUDING ART, DESIGN, SCIENCE, AND TECHNOLOGY.

How would you describe Kyoto?
Kyoto is one of Japan's living treasures. Nature is present everywhere here. We're surrounded by mountains and next to the biggest lake in Japan. But even though Kyoto is known for the beauty of its monuments and culture, the latter is unfortunately difficult to preserve and protect.

Yet you epitomize Kyoto's arts and crafts and seem to be flourishing ...
Today, maybe ... but that wasn't the case 15 years ago. At the time, there seemed to be no future for the ancestral skills our houses represented. Our parents didn't want us to invest our lives in them. There was no hope or money there.
When we were 20, we decided to join forces to try and change the mindset and mentality around arts and crafts. *Go On* was born out of our desire to share our knowhow with children so they

would want to become artisans. Like giving them a dream to shoot for!
We organize exhibitions, participate in debates, and create events.

What is your philosophy?

We remain rooted in respect for our craft and, together, nurture the emotions that guide us.

What areas of Kyoto would you recommend?

Outside Kyoto, spend a night by Lake Biwa in Shiga Prefecture. Or in Ine and Amanohashidate on the Sea of Japan, making sure to pass through Tamba on the way.
Behind the Kaikado shop, Kyoto's old red-light district also has a certain appeal, with a lovely canal and an old cookie factory to discover.

Otherwise, we really like the spot where the two rivers meet, as well as Arashiyama, which is a very interesting mix of nature and temples, though it's also more touristy. And then, of course, there's the must-have experience of climbing Mount Daimonji!

One last tip for enjoying Kyoto even more.

If we want everyone to be able to enjoy Kyoto for a long time to come, let's all start by protecting it! It's easy, really: just don't do anything in Kyoto that you wouldn't do at home.
Visit our city in a quiet and respectful way. Come meet us – we'd love to talk to you and exchange ideas!

Kaikado	tea canisters	kaikado.jp
Kochosai Kosuga	bamboo	en.kohchosai.co.jp
Hosoo	silk	hosoo-kyoto.com
Nakagawa Mokkugei	wood	kogeistandard.com
Kanaami Tsuji	metal	kanaamitsuji.net
Asahiyaki Ware	pottery	asahiyaki.com

GO TREASURE HUNTING
AND EAT A VEGAN PASTRY
OR TWO

An oasis in Kyoto ... It's impossible to enter Stardust without feeling enveloped in a sense of wellbeing, far from the hubbub of the outside world, which suddenly feels miles away.

Welcome to a gourmet vegan café that will help you make peace with certain principles and benefits of this diet. And once you've eaten your fill, you can start hunting for pottery, clothes, and other vintage items.

 STARDUST
41 SHICHIKU SHIMOTAKEDONOCHO,
KITA-KU

京都市北区紫竹下竹殿町 41

| DAILY: 11am / 6pm EXCEPT MON & THU: Closed | +81 75-286-7296 | stardustkyoto.com Reservation required for the café |

A TIMELESS
BRUNCH EXPERIENCE

Whatever you do, don't miss the brunch at Farmoon, one of Kyoto's most exclusive and unique restaurants.

Get ready for a transformative, one-of-a-kind experience ... We don't want to spoil the joy of discovery for you, so we'll leave it at that.

 FARMOON
9 KITASHIRAKAWA HIGASHIKUBOTACHO
SAKYO-KU

京都市左京区 北白川東久保田町 9

Opening days vary, check on Instagram:	Reservation required via info@farmoon.kyoto.jp
noon / 5pm	Instagram @farmoon_kyoto
MON–WED: Closed	

AN ANTIQUES STORE
WITH SECRETS

Where the spirit of Paris's Saint-Ouen and London's Portobello Road flea markets finds its way into the streets of Kyoto ...

Sowgen is a unique place where you'll love hunting for the soul of Japan. And then, between the cluttered alleys, the most adorable tea room will suddenly appear, as if by magic.

Take the time to stop by: exploring its nooks and crannies will teach you all about the beauty of this country.

📍 **SOWGEN**
573 TAKAMIYACHO, NAKAGYO-KU

京都市中京区高宮町573

TUE–SUN: 11:30am / 7:30pm
MON and 2ND WED of each month: closed

+81 75-252-1007

sowgen.com
instagram: @sowgen_shijo

LIKE BEING A GUEST
IN SOMEONE'S HOME

Everyone dreams of opening the door to a real Japanese home to discover everyday life within its walls and meet the owner.

Totousha makes this dream come true. Just make an appointment and immerse yourself in traditional Japanese culture: book a tea ceremony, a calligraphy course, or a Noh theater workshop ... Anything is possible here. Tarek will welcome you and share his passion for his culture.

For a truly exceptional excursion, ask him to take you on a tour of the surrounding temples.

 TOTOUSHA
63-38 MURASAKINO DAITOKUJICHO,
KITA-KU

北区紫野大徳寺町63-38

+81 90-4616-3887 | On request: totousha.com

© MARIANO WECHSLER

- KIKI GEISSE -

AN EXPERT IN JAPANESE CULTURE, KIKI GEISSE HAS BEEN DEVOTING HERSELF
TO THE JAPANESE TEA CEREMONY FOR 12 YEARS.

Kiki-san, what is your relationship with Kyoto?

I came here to study tea, which allowed me to discover people and places that are not usually easy to access. It was a magical experience that filled me with a constant sense of wonder.

Kyoto is a very special city. The pace here is very slow compared to Tokyo, for example. When you come to Kyoto you have to try to slide into this rhythm, this slowness. To enjoy the city, you have to be patient, to observe and feel rather than consume the sights like a tourist - instead of trying to visit five temples a day or get the perfect Instagram shot, you have to live in the moment and connect with each place instead. It has to be a conscious act.

In your opinion, what's the best way to enjoy Kyoto?

Definitely by bike! Use the river as your central axis and cycle up north to Kamigamo temple and down south to 7th Street by Kaikado Café (they have excellent tea cocktails). From this axis, take byways and detours depending on what areas you want to visit. Kyoto may have been largely destroyed, but there's still so much to discover!

You co-created Totousha and gave it life for four years. Tell us about your experience.

We were three young graduates who wanted to find a way to put the tea culture we'd learned into practice. It's important to understand that not many people in Japan have room for this. We created an initial event open to the public to call attention to Kyoto's public baths, which are under threat. Based on how it resonated in the media, we realized that everyone misses and wants to connect with each other and to the roots of our traditions. Kyoto is a very closed city, even for its own inhabitants!

That was the beginning of the Totousha adventure: an explosion of freedom, creativity, and encounters with people of all ages, cultures, and backgrounds. We mixed genres and thought about how to anchor each part of our culture in contemporary life.

Walking through Totousha's door is an intimate experience, unlike entering a museum or gallery. It allows you to understand traditional life and culture by giving you the feeling that you're joining and becoming part of a community.

PUBLIC BATHS CONVERTED
INTO A CAFÉ

While the tragedy of the slow and silent disappearance of Kyoto's public baths is sadly very real, the locals' ingenuity in preserving these sites is luckily very much alive. At Sarasa, they've been turned into a peaceful gourmet haven.

Stop by for a well-deserved break and make sure to try the lemon pie, which alone is worth the trip.

SARASA NISHIJIN CAFÉ
11-1 MURASAKINO HIGASHIFUJINOMORICHO, KITA-KU

京都市北区紫野東藤ノ森町11-1
さらさ西陣

| DAILY: noon / 10pm | +81 75-432-5075 | cafe-sarasa.com |

THE BEST
SUNSET

In the heart of the Gion district, by the river, there's a terrace unlike any other. It's *the* spot for taking in the sunset while sipping a cocktail, far from the hustle and bustle of the city.

Much more enjoyable than the beer gardens that pop up on the rooftops of Kyoto in spring, Y Roof throws together people of all generations and cultures against a backdrop of laughter.

 Y ROOF
19 BENZAITENCHO, HIGASHIYAMA WARD
Y GION BUILDING, 6th floor

 京都市東山区弁財天町19 4F

| Only open for events: see calendar on website | +81 75-533-8555 | ygion.com |

ELECTRO MUSIC
BY CANDLELIGHT

Unnamed bar, the bar without a name: don't be surprised that it's difficult to find – that's part of the concept!

Good luck locating it on your first try …

But it's worth the effort when what awaits you is a cutting-edge selection of electro music in a bar lit only by candles and open until all hours.

 UNNAMED BAR
309 BIZENJIMACHO, NAKAGYO WARD,
3rd floor, above Elefant Factory Coffee

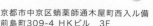

京都市中京区蛸薬師通木屋町西入ル備
前島町309-4 HKビル　3F

DAILY: from 9pm

A MAGICAL NIGHT
TWO HOURS FROM KYOTO

Craving a big breath of fresh air? A break in your hectic sightseeing schedule?

There's a traditional house just two hours outside of Kyoto that's perfect for recharging your batteries. Located in Ine, a fishing village on the Sea of Japan, this house is part of a crazy global itinerant hotel project.

Carefully considered and dedicated hospitality that's perfectly suited to the passage of time.

 700'000 HEURES
EBISUYA, 896 KAMESHIMA,
INE-CHO, YOZA-GUN

えびす屋京都府与謝郡伊根町亀島896

Open April to October

700000heures.com
contact@700000heures.com

© SHIN JINUSHI

In the *Soul of* collection, the 31st address
is never revealed because it's top secret.
We leave it up to you to find it.

THE SECRET
ADDRESS

Locate Kuramaguchi Street on a map. Find a temple known for its restaurant devoted to Buddhist cuisine (here's a hint: there's a white plaster arch at the entrance) .... Walk around it to the left and discover the secrets of the lair that awaits you. *Kanpai!*

 Starting point:
KURAMAGUCHI STREET

DAILY: 5pm / 9pm